KARMA

WHAT REVIEWERS SAY

At a time where the ground has suddenly and literally seismically shifted beneath us, we need to focus on what really matters. This book brings you key principles to help us to re-center on that which is truly important; the people we interact with and how we can make a difference in this world.

—Mark Bryant, Partner IBM

Joanne's book will help you get real and through these times. And yes, to somewhere better. Crisis is the call for the best of you to step forward. Karma will help you do so successfully.
—Cathy Johnson, President Asia Professional Speakers, Singapore

This is an eminently practical book that offers not just hope but a pathway to real solutions, to wellbeing, at the individual, family, team, company, community, and country level. It's a leadership book, a culture book, a strategy book, a performance book, a book of value all wrapped in the package of kindness, compassion, and empathy. We need this book right now.

—Dave Cooper, former Navy SEAL

A warm, upward path during a time of rude awakening.

—Kat van Zutphen, design thinker

A practical and straight from the heart book on using ourselves to good to create the world we want even in crisis.

—Wendy Tan, author of *Wholeness in a Disruptive World*

Reading Karma is like having an enlightening conversation with a best friend over a calming mug of hot chocolate. It's the perfect companion to elevate your spirit and spark a virtuous cycle through inspired action. An uplifting read!

—Karen Leong, Director, Influence Solutions
and author of *Win People Over*

We have moved from rhetoric to reality, where transformation is no longer a buzzword and is the top survival skill of our times. Packed full of tips, tools and powerful reframing questions, Karma is a much needed message to help you navigate these and move to create a kinder, more purposeful tomorrow.

—Natalie Turner, Speaker, Creator of The Six 'I's®
and author of *Yes, You Can Innovate*.

This is for: *executives, entrepreneurs, and business leaders*

Why this book: *focused impulse to help you in these troubled, turbulent, torrid times*

KARMA

How to Stay **Calm** and **Productive**
from Crisis to the Recovery

Joanne Flinn

the Business Growth Lady

Author: Joanne Flinn
Editor: Louisa Bennion
Layout: Karl Hunt
Illustrator: Booth Aster

All rights reserved. 2nd edition 2020

ISBN: 978-0-9943233-9-2

To you, out there changing the world for the better
during this crisis—particularly the nurses, doctors,
and scientists on the front line

Contents

Why Now

I write this while in the middle of the Covid-19 outbreak for my friend and colleague, Joanne. My wife and I are sheltering in place, and physical distancing is now a neighborhood skill set. In a matter of days, we all have lost our freedoms and liberties. There is no immediate end in sight to this condition.

We all are asking the same question: "What does it take to get through this crisis and come out the other side in better shape?" Joanne's book of *33 Karma Action Points* provides a full spectrum offer of guidance for us. She helps us think about how we show up, what we do, our family, money, work, kindness and more. This is a book that will activate your best version of yourself and call you into actions that benefit other people.

This is a book of practice. Pick one of the karma action points that appeals to you and for the next twenty-four hours, use that element to gently serve yourself and others as best you can. If it is true that we are in this crisis together—and I believe it to be so—then Joanne's book provides the binding material we need to thicken our human connections and come through this crisis together.

Rick Torseth
Chairman of the Change Leaders
CEO, Human Securities

March 23, 2020
Bainbridge Island, Washington

What Happened

Crisis. Plans have to change. This year is not the year any of us planned.

Me, I'd just released the book *Karma In Action—how to use karma and kindness for business success*. It's about resilience, positive psychology, and practical business action, and it's drawn from my MSc days at HEC Paris and Saïd Business School at the University of Oxford. It's a modern take on well-respected ancient wisdom.

With the outbreak of COVID-19, I'm pivoting and reassessing, like all of you, and what was to be a book launch month has become my chance to help you find spaces for kindness and moments of calm in these troubled times.

As the novel coronavirus spreads, with its ever-changing impact on lives and businesses, here are 33 concrete actions you (and your team) can take to cultivate resiliency and a positive psychology for business performance.

These last few weeks have been full-on for all of us. Every plan that I had for 2020 has been turned on its head. Q1, normally the quarter where we find our footing for the new year, is the quarter where it went upside down. I've had to make very real choices on how to act in uncertain times, both as a leader and as businessperson.

At the personal level, I've had had family member in ICU on medical, oxygen, and feeding tubes for a fortnight. Ten days ago, I got a phone call: "Can you be here in 15 minutes? He might not make it." My sister and my niece picked me up and we went in. The ICU disinfectant smell settled into my nostrils as, one by one, family gathered—all ten of us.

When the nurses took the life-support tubes out . . . he kept breathing. He is now on the road to recovery.

In writing this now, I feel very blessed that it was possible to live through this moment together. Ten days later, we'd not be allowed in. My heart goes out to everyone with loved ones in ICU that they can't see.

During this time, I've watched my brain melt down and I've had to recover it and focus on those around me, on what I can do for them. I've drawn on decades of learning. When the emotions hit, I'm simply rolling with them and then when it's calm, getting onto things.

It's a roller coaster. I reflect on my younger self. She'd have wanted to control it all and tell people what they should do.

She'd have used anger and power to try and hold the fear at bay. She would not have been able to deal with all these emotions. They were things that were dangerous and to be well repressed and buried. I was so in control as a leader, my feelings were dead. I was a robot. I was a road warrior.

The cost of this, not just to me but to those around me—my team, my clients and my family—hit when I was running a multi-million-dollar business for PricewaterhouseCoopers. It took a crisis much like the one we face to today for me to realize I had to do things differently. I needed a new mind-set. I needed a new heartset. I needed them in that moment, and I needed them to build for recovery and a better future.

Do you have your own stories of meltdown? Of trying to be strong? Of seeing someone loose it? Of seeing the dark side of the human spirit in the hoarding and pushing others aside? Have you seen the bright side show up, too?

Now, as important as it is to manage our mindsets for resilience and positive psychology, let's also be real: many businesses have two to six weeks of cash flow. As much as we focus on keeping ourselves and our loved ones alive through this crisis, we also care about our businesses, the people they serve, and the good they can do if they stay alive, too.

This book is for you as an individual human, and it's also for you as a leader of others, as someone who has responsibly either as an executive or entrepreneur or as someone who manages their own P&L—or their family P&L.

I firmly believe business can be a force for good. How we as business leaders show up **right now** makes a difference not only during the crisis, but in the world that we create in recovery.

When my first crisis hit, 15 years ago, robot mode didn't work. The old rules of management didn't work. The hero-on-a-burning-platform routine didn't work. I had to discover what it took to keep a team together, serving clients and coming out strong even when 90% of our cash flow collapsed. The rich were selling Mercedes and Rolexes to keep afloat. I learnt about the **real** nine capitals of business. These are as valid today in the days of unicorns, uncertainty, and COVID-19 as they were when I was successfully shepherding people and businesses through the Asian financial crisis, the dotcom bust, 9/11, SARS and the global financial crisis of 2008.

What do I mean by "successfully?" I mean I was doing better, both as a person and as a business leader.

I had to go back to something I'd learned as a child. My family moved a lot. I'd lived through five revolutions and on five continents by the time I was twelve. I saw people starve. There was violence and social collapse. What got my family through was kindness.

> *Kindness: apparently small simple acts of consideration for someone else.*

It's kindness that helps you to stay calm, centered, and active for the greater good.

The power of this simple principle was challenged during 9/11 and even more so through SARS, when fear of infection and death took over.

Kindness will help you and your business to keep running and building a future now, as fear runs high and worry for loved ones and for our own ability to stay afloat dominates our thoughts.

Kindness is a valid path to get through crisis, it will help you to get to the recovery. It will help you create a new world.

Joanne Flinn

How To Use This Book

This book is deliberately structured as a book to dip into. Pick a section, open a page. Each of the sections is short and self-contained, a piece to help you, your mindset, those around you, and—yes, your business.

The Science Behind It All

Underpinning this book is sound science. In addition to my 25 years of doing business, dealing with crises and leading transformation, some years ago I did a Master of Science at HEC Paris and Saïd Business School at the University of Oxford. During this time, I co-founded the Change Leaders, a global community of professionals focusing on leadership, uncertainty, and disruption. This is a deep think tank of experts who live and breathe resilience, positive psychology, neuroscience, turbulence, scenarios, sense-making, and other technical change leadership expertise. We regularly engage with other experts from Harvard, Saïd and HEC. I say this not to impress you but to reassure you: what's here is firmly, profoundly grounded.

ONCE I NEW ONLY DARKNESS AND STILLNESS ... MY LIFE WAS WITHOUT PAST OR FUTURE ... BUT A LITTLE WORD FROM THE FINGERS OF ANOTHER FELL INTO MY HAND THAT CLUTCHED AT EMPTINESS, AND MY HEART LEAPED TO THE RAPTURE OF LIVING.

—Helen Keller

WHO YOU ARE

Let's start positive. I want to feed your mind with what could be, and what you can do now. I call this the Unicorning Manifesto: it's the call for the magnificence in you not only shine but also to leap into action. After all, if not now, when?

Kindness begins with you. It's got three parts: your intention + your receiver + your action. *Your receiver?* I hear you ask. Yes, kindness needs someone on the receiving end. That someone might be as small and close as a friend or as enormous as the climate and the planet. It could also be *you*.

As big as the COVID-19 crisis is right now, we've also got the climate crisis and other things to work on if we want a better world.

Our mindset needs to acknowledge the power of what is still possible, even if right now things are not easy.

No One Should Tell You It Can't Be Done

Follow the laws, be thoughtful about others—and keep your dreams and vision alive for what you are creating. While it might be more difficult right now, see what's happening as:

1. A storm—this too will pass
2. A new wind—which will blow good things your way
3. An opportunity—now find it!

Avoid: Saying it can't be done.

Ask: What would be helpful to move things forward at this moment?

Do: Keep your big vision up and visible and encourage others.

IN A GENTLE WAY, YOU CAN SHAKE THE WORLD.

—Mahatma Gandi

Serious Fun is Fabulous

My inner robot struggled with this. *Be serious,* I was told. However, in times of crisis, seriousness can trigger fear and worry and get you stuck in a downward spiral. Yes, it's a balancing act between looking at the facts of what's happening—and aiming into the future.

This is where serious fun comes in.[1] It's also good neuroscience, as it helps you produce serotonin, dopamine, and other brain goodies. When your brain has these in abundance, there is space for insight, innovation, and constructive contribution—all of which are highly necessary right now.

Watch for your serious mode. It shows up in:

1. Your voice
2. Your fears
3. Critical assessments

---

1 Great leaders use fun to lighten the emotional load of stress and seriousness. Good-hearted fun, please.

Avoid: Critical mode

Ask: Given what we know now, what else needs consideration?

Do: Share the fun and the good things that are also happening with others who might be struggling with too much seriousness.

ONCE WE BELIEVE IN OURSELVES, WE CAN RISK CURIOSITY, WONDER, SPONTANEOUS DELIGHT, OR ANY EXPERIENCE THAT REVEALS THE HUMAN SPIRIT

—e e cummings

It's Time for Unicorning

Everything around us was once impossible. The people who think differently, the crazy ones who dream and who deal with the disruptions that take them off the path—they're the ones who've put in the work and added something better to our world.

Even . . . ugh, the guy who first invented fire (yeah, it's a little too soon, if you're from Australia).

Now is the moment to put the explosion of time, energy, and space that quarantine has created for us into unicorning. Now's your chance to focus on doing something that is magnificent, meaningful, and valuable.

With what's going on across the planet, there are so many opportunities to help and so many problems to solve, all of which can make a better world.

Be inspired by **Canva,** who started out helping the rest of us do better graphic design. And by **Xero,** whose business and accounting software has helped millions look after their businesses. Insider secret: they both do kindness well.

Avoid: Dismissing other's ideas as not valuable.

Ask: If this was for a billion people, what would be a simple beginning?

Do: Help a company do their business better with your best genius.

YOU MUST DO THE THINGS YOU THINK YOU CANNOT DO.

—Eleanor Roosevelt

It's Not Just Time to Unicorn, it's Time for Wings

What are wings for? Wings get you where you want to go faster.

Factoids:

- Jets are three time faster than the fastest land vehicle.
- Golden falcons are three times faster than cheetahs.

If you are going to go for it, go all the way. If what you are doing is good, go for magnificence. At this unique moment, why limit yourself just to the *possible*? Note, this is about commitment not about current cash.

To whet your taste buds . . . what if your actions could help 100 other businesses? What if this helps 1,000 families? As you move forward, what if women got paid equally to men? What if men were given the same space to be fathers as women traditionally hold as parents? What if you did your magnificence in a way that made the climate better and the planet healthier along the way?

One of the interesting side-effects of the spread of the coronavirus is that pollution levels have come down. What if you build for recovery that means a pollution-free or climate-positive future?

What excites you?

Excitement gives you wings. Kindness gives you wings.

> **Avoid:** Sticking to the logical limits of reasonable.
>
> **Ask:** What would be magnificent?
>
> **Do:** Help someone do something faster.

START BY DOING WHAT'S NECESSARY; THEN DO WHAT'S POSSIBLE AND SUDDENLY YOU ARE DOING THE IMPOSSIBLE.

—Francis of Assisi

Do Good, Make Money, Repeat

Having spent years in businesses that focused on the money first, I'll admit I missed something important. **First** create value. **First** do good. Then money is an outcome. This is as true for business metrics as it is for life.

Doing good is like looking forward to create the future you want. It might be the future you want in five minutes, or the future you want as we recover from this global crisis.

Focusing on money first is like looking though the rear-view mirror.

Note: *for the CFOs reading this, look at the section on money.*

Avoid: Focusing on what is in the past—it's just what it was.

Ask: What would I really like? Who do I know that would really like this too?

Do: Give this to them in some way, even if it is small.

Note 2: *If money is what you want, then give money to someone who needs it. Do it with care and consideration, in a way that helps and respects them.*

For example, some years ago when my funds were super tight, I got on a bus with $2 left in my wallet. Two tourists got on the bus and discovered they were $2 short of what they needed for their fares. I gave them my $2, which was all I had at the time, so I had to trust I'd be fine. And that evening, unexpectedly, someone treated me to dinner. This is the principle of Karma in Action—in action.

HOW WONDERFUL IT IS THAT NOBODY NEED WAIT A SINGLE MOMENT BEFORE STARTING TO IMPROVE THE WORLD.

—Anne Frank

Design for Change, Build for People

Uncertainty, volatility, disruption, and ambiguity are all part of our business lexicon. We know this, and yet many businesses and teams design only for stability. COVID-19 shows us how real disruption is.

As you design the future, who you are right now, and what you want for yourself as the global recovery gets underway, design for change. Design for adaptation. Design for agility.

Design as a unicorn. The real way forward attracts people, creates joy, and shows courage.

Build so it's human, respectful, and compassionate. Keep in mind that what you do to others comes back to you.

We know there will be twists and turns. We're all riding the edges of chaos right now. The deepest insights of those who've studied crises and gotten to the other side of chaos is this: design so that the organization (which might mean your family) can change and adapt, be consistent with your core value, and be good to others.[2]

> **Avoid:** Adding complexity, sub-rules, and conditions.
>
> **Ask:** How can we make this simpler? What is the essence of what we are after?
>
> **Do:** Pause, take a moment and help someone get to the simplicity of what's really important. It's the flip side of complexity.

IF OPPORTUNITY DOESN'T KNOCK, BUILD A DOOR.

—Milton Berle

---

2 Richard Pascale wrote a great book on this called *Surfing on the Edge of Chaos*. I spoke with him some years ago at Oxford and remain in awe of the calm, centered simplicity of his work. When things get complex, it's time to go to the simple principles that work.

WHAT WE THINK,
WE BECOME.

—Buddha

Stand for Kindness, Sustainability, and Equity

At the risk of playing hardball, what sort of world do you want? One of toxicity and disruption? One where you and your children cannot breath? One where your daughter is paid 25% less than your son, causing her to struggle financially and face hardship in her old age?

Or one where there is kindness. Where the climate and planet are in balance. Where both your daughter and your son are valued and respected equally.

We are leaders in making the world we want. Our actions can and will make this possible, and we can do it now. Even in the context of a pandemic, we can make choices that lead to this better future.

The facts are simple: every month we delay addressing these big issues of our times is another month for the damage caused by those issues to compound. As we are seeing with the spread of the coronavirus, the sooner action is taken, the smaller the impact and the swifter the recovery.

Weirdly, pandemic is giving us the opportunity to reset how we do things. Let's not waste this chance.

> **Avoid:** Focusing on the tree; we also need to deal with the other challenges in the forest.
>
> **Ask:** What actions can we take that advance all four together: recovery, kindness, sustainability, and equity?
>
> **Do:** Check each decision, and help your colleagues do so too.

Business talk: supply chains are being re-tooled as COVID-19 continues to impact more businesses, and families, and regions. One current challenge is that businesses have learned to optimize their supply chains to be lean and thin. Thin, lean, highly optimized supply chains are rarely resilient. Resilience was, sadly, not a factor to be taken into account in the optimization parameters. It's time to move past simply optimizing for capital and customers.

We Are Building the Better Future

What other future should we build? We've been given a pause, a chance to contemplate what we do. While I acknowledge and feel the stress and the fear the pandemic is creating, I'm also mindful, like any leader who has been through crisis, that it's an opportunity to do things differently. To do things better. To put the time and energy that is now available into doing something good.

In practical terms, how many hours are now freed up to design, plan, and build something better? How can we use this moment to identify and solve the meaningful problems of our day?

Avoid: Wasting the time, energy, and passion that could be harnessed for constructive action.

Ask: What is the highest and best use of the energy available to us right now?

Do: Put your energy into constructive action: now is the time for projects.

Both **Google** and **Atlassian** have done a lot of good and cre-ated great businesses by allotting 5% of their workers' time as "free time" where staff had the freedom to create things they thought would help customers, community, and business.

You've a treasure of time and potential innovation at your fingertips. Use it well.

"DON'T WASTE A GOOD CRISIS."

—*Sir Winston Churchill*

IT IS DURING OUR DARKEST MOMENTS THAT WE MUST FOCUS TO SEE THE LIGHT.

—Aristotle

MEMORIES OF OUR LIVES, OF OUR WORKS AND OUR DEEDS WILL CONTINUE IN OTHERS.

—*Rosa Parks*

WHAT WE DO

Let's take what we do deeper. Our actions, our words and, yes, our thoughts create the future. They also create how we feel right now.

From a space of kindness, there are three elements in the *WHAT* that we do.

1. Your intention: the essence of what you want
2. Your receiver: who you are doing it for
3. Your action: what you actually do

You also need to pay attention to the emotional context in which you and those close to you are operating. This changes from moment to moment. I've seen it in my own roller coaster.

To depersonalize that emotional space, and in the spirit of serious fun, its regions are:

1. The Land of the Impossible
2. The Land of Dreams
3. The Land of Discipline
4. The Land of the Unicorn

Your Intention

Have you ever had someone give you a gift and felt that there was something mean behind it? On the other hand, has someone ever done something wonderful for you simply out of sincerity and care? Did you feel the difference?

We can delve into the science of mirror neurons and heart math, but the simple truth is that we can feel what others intend.

So, when you are intending to be kind, hold the feeling in both your head and your heart.

And if you want to super-charge it, be clear about your intention to help. Be clear that your help is meant to give its recipient the essence of what they are looking for.

Avoid: Assuming that what you want is what other people want.

Ask: What would really be of service?

Do: Listen actively for the other person's deeper meaning, and support that.

TO THE MIND THAT IS STILL, THE WHOLE UNIVERSE SURRENDERS.

—Lao Tzu

Your Receiver

It's simple: kindness is not really about you. It's about who you are being kind to, and what will help them.

Have you ever had someone offer to help you, only to find out there were all sorts of strings attached?

Kindness is powerful when it's given cleanly and without expectation.

Right now, many people are in overwhelm and they can't tell you what they need. You may need to watch, observe, and have empathy to work out what would be really helpful.

Avoid: Pushing your own agenda.

Ask: What can I give that is meaningful NOW and easy to receive?

Do: Observe, pay attention, and be considerate.

For example: late last year a friend was looking after her aunt during her final days. She recounted that the best help was not from people saying, "Tell me what you need." Her mind was full of what was happening. The best help was from those who were active, who said they'd organize something like regular meals, and got it happening.

NO ACT OF KINDNESS, NO MATTER HOW SMALL, IS EVER WASTED.

—Aesop

AND WHEN I BREATHED, MY BREATH WAS LIGHTNING.

—*Black Elk*

Your Action

You've got your heart and thoughts aligned with your intention and you are focused on your receiver and what they need . . . now it's time to take action.

Do it.

A thousand plans come to nothing if no action is taken. Take that step. Do it.

Avoid: Avoiding doing things or overthinking them.

Ask: What can I do now? (Not later, not when things are calm or perfect.)

Do: Do it. Now.

In the Land of the Impossible

With all their fears and uncertainties amidst a global pandemic and its economic impact, the person you want to help may be in the land of the impossible.

Impossible is where things can't happen. If we stay in this place for too long, it turns into the land of broken dreams.

It may feel like overwhelm or exhaustion, like it can't be done or it's too hard. Psychologically, this is a valid response. It could be a signal to rest and recover. When things don't work out, everything can feel impossible.

Be ok and recognize that this occurs. If the person lost in the land of the impossible is you, be kind to yourself.

Avoid: Judging fear and uncertainty as bad or wrong. It simply is.

Ask: Is there something simple that we could do? Try to bring this person some simple pleasure.

For example, to go for a walk, or to play music. In a quarantine situation, a phone call, video message, email, or text can go a long way to fight that person's sense of isolation in the land of the impossible.

Do: Reach out in kindness.

Note 1: *When fear drives a sense of impossibility, it's a destructive space. Adrenal glands are hijacking our frontal cortex, which where deep thinking occurs. Cortisol buzzes through our system. For short spurts, this buzz can be useful. For extended periods, it's better to do simple, kind things.*

Note 2: *In the creativity space, downtime is a powerful period for insight. It's best used in reflection, meditation, relaxation, and revitalization. And then take deliberate action to find possibilities, small pleasures, and enjoyment.*

AND THE DAY CAME WHEN THE RISK TO REMAIN TIGHT IN A BUD WAS MORE PAINFUL THAN THE RISK IT TOOK TO BLOSSOM

—Anaïs Nin

TIME STAYS LONG ENOUGH FOR ANYONE WHO WILL USE IT

—Leonardo da Vinci

In the Land of Dreams

As the mind begins to relax, possibilities start again. Here, kindness is about focusing on constructive dreams, on what could be better.

The key here is to come from a positive intention to build better rather than a space of complaint and judgment that presumes others are doing things wrong.

Avoid: Complaining or seeing others as wrong.

Ask: What might be possible?

Do: Sketch it out. Draw models and create prototypes.

All great creative insights have an *aha* moment, that 5% of inspiration. And it usually takes many iterations to refine the insight. For example, many of the ideas in this book are ones I developed over the years through keynote speaking and the process of writing my previous books.

In the Land of Discipline

Inspiration evaporates if no effort is made to embody it—which brings us to the 95% perspiration that necessary to get things done. We are in new times, and COVID-19 is creating a situation that none of us have seen before.

So, as you go about taking step-by-step actions that make sense, be kind to those around you and to yourself. Things are going differently than expected for all of us. Some things may be harder. But certain unicorn-spirited people are also finding ways to help and resolve some of the challenges.

It is going to be a process of trying something, seeing what works, and adapting. It will be a zigzag. We may need to take steps to the side or even backwards in order to move forward.

Avoid: Giving people a hard time when things aren't working out.

Ask: What can we learn and refine?

Do: Encourage people to try new approaches.

Bonus karma points for the land of discipline. Take breaks and celebrate each time you achieve something, even if that something is learning. See also the next section on fear of failure.

ALL WORK IS EMPTY SAVE WHERE THERE IS LOVE

—*Khalil Gibran*

I DO NOT SEEK.
I FIND.

—Pablo Picasso

KARMA ACTION POINT 15

In the Land of the Unicorn

You've found your rhythm in the zig zag of progress and discovery. While today's world is not a fluffy space where all is good news and light, you'll find our current condition, too, can eventually be a space of exhilaration and adventure.

Things are happening. Movement. Results. The next space of opportunity opens.

And yes, sometimes your path will take you back to the other lands. Remember, each has its value. Through the course of this crisis and the eventual recovery, each realm helps us create a better future.

Avoid: Hubris and ego of saying *we've got this.*

Ask: What can we do next to help?

Do: Do good. Give forward.

I'VE BEEN ABSOLUTELY
TERRIFIED EVERY MOMENT OF
MY LIFE – AND I'VE NEVER LET IT
KEEP ME FROM DOING A SINGLE
THING I WANTED TO DO.

—*Georgia O'Keefe*

DEALING WITH THE FEAR VIRUS

The novel coronavirus is a very real threat to our health. For the elderly and immunocompromised, this is particularly true. But the bigger threat to our world is the fear virus. Its spread is a thousand times more virulent, and it's very, very hard to wash our hands of it. It shuts down thinking, compassion, and kindness.

It creates fights over toilet rolls. Runs on eggs. Border shutdowns. Shortages of food, and shortages of patience, particularly in families confined together for weeks on end. It will leave business and personal bankruptcy in its wake, as business slows down and jobs are lost. Yes, it's bad. It's horrid.

So let me ask you, do you want to live in fear?

No?

Well, let's talk about how to stop spreading *that* virus.

I HAVE DECIDED TO STICK WITH LOVE. HATE IS TOO GREAT A BURDEN TO BEAR.

—Martin Luther King, Jr

Fear is the Mind Killer

When I first read Frank Herbert's *Dune*, I didn't get it. I do now. I can perceive how the feeling of fear floods my mind. How it goes into a log jam that a beaver would be proud of. That my ability to think rationally is stuck. This is a standard neurological response.

Act to reduce the fear. At its most fundamental level, fear is a story we are telling ourselves about what could happen. It's not actually real *right now*.

Avoid: Spreading fear, rumors, doubts, and worries.

Ask: Is what I'm afraid of really real *right now* in this moment I'm in?

Do: Breath in deeply. Breath out deeply. Do this three times. Deliberately change your mental story.

This is a practice from the cognitive behavioral world.

Advanced practices: mindfulness and meditation.

Do Calm

As you calm down or as you help someone nearby to calm down, notice what is actually happening around you.

For example: a valid fear is a sabre-tooth tiger about to attack you.

For many of us right now, when we take the moment to be calm and look around, there are actually some lovely things happening. Singing from balconies in Sicily, water ways clearing in Venice, blue skies over Guanzhao are just the beginning.

Avoid: Presuming it is all bad and expecting things to go wrong. (At the same time, avoid telling other people to calm down.)

Ask: What can I seen around me? What can I learn from this?

Do: Appreciate the good that continues happening all around you. If you want to help someone else appreciate it, say: breathe with me for a minute. Let's just feel our breath.

The fact is, the more you manage to be calm and appreciative of all the good that is here, the more you'll see those things, almost as if you were making them happen just by noticing. The mental filters we call the reticular activating system will highlight things that match what you're hoping to see. It's a virtuous feedback loop that can do wonders for your well-being.

LEADERSHIP IS GAINING THE CONFIDENCE TO PUT LOVE OVER EGO.

—*Katya Andresen*

IT'S FINE TO CELEBRATE SUCCESS BUT IT IS MORE IMPORTANT TO HEED THE LESSONS OF FAILURE.

—*Bill Gates*

FACTS

If you are going to share information, fact-check first. Get verified data. This is not the time for fake news, fearmongering, or scarifying, even when the source appears credible.

What does fact-checking look like? It means clicking the links, going down through the rabbit warren of the internet till you get to a real journalistic source. As you read the source, evaluate its interpretation for bias and credibility.

Once you've done all that, reflect on point you wish to make by sharing this particular news item on social media. Consider whether it adds to people's calmness and well-being or to their overall knowledge. If the answer is no, why are you sharing? Another good practice is to provide a brief summary or commentary on any news item you share. If you find you can't provide some meaningful original content in the form of interpretation, maybe there's nothing worth sharing in that particular item!

Find sites that share facts and speak calmly. My preferred ones at the moment are:

> *www.worldmeters.info for global data*
>
> *https://www.weforum.org/ for global coverage*
>
> *https://www.moh.gov.sg/covid-19 is my local ministry of health in Singapore (wherever you are, find yours)*
>
> *https://www.health.gov.au/news/health-alerts/novel-COVID19virus-2019-ncov-health-alert/COVID19virus-covid-19-current-situation-and-case-numbers helps me keep tabs on my family in Australia (wherever your loved ones live, find the local/regional/national site that will keep you informed)*

I'm also following commentators like **Andrea T Edwards** whose message for courage and leadership resonates strongly with me. **Dave Cooper** writes sensible change leadership articles that deal with both fear and facts.

Facts, not fear, are the food we need right now.

Validate Facts

In the business world, we rely on facts and figures to help us make the best decisions. However, arriving at and agreeing on one version of the truth is harder than ever right now.

Here are some useful sites to help you sharpen your fact-checking skills:

https://www.ifla.org/publications/node/11174

https://www.summer.harvard.edu/inside-summer/4-tips-spotting-fake-news-story

Make sure you consult sources that give you different perspectives—this will help create wiser, better outcomes. There is a very real possibility of GroupThink, where narrow, self-re-enforcing perspectives dominate our discourse. The challenges we face today call for multi-perspective solutions: ones that address both health issues and economic impacts, and also help reduce other issues that are still important, even if they are not in the forefront of our minds.

> **Avoid:** Fact fiction, making it up or not checking. Don't help fake news spread.
>
> **Ask:** How can I ensure this is real information that is worth sharing?
>
> **Do:** Share reliable, verified information.

FACTS ... STAND FORTH IN NAKED AND SIMPLE BEAUTY.

—*Galileo Galilei*

Priorities Persist

While we are on the topic of data, this leads us (indirectly) to themes of fear and priorities. Let's take a step back from the pandemic staring us in the face and take a look at society's attitude toward another disease.

The preventable, curable disease malaria killed 405,000 people last year. My sincere hope is that both COVID-19 and malaria are cured. Both create tragedy for individuals and families.

To date, the World Bank has committed $14 billion[3] to deal with the impact of COVID-19 while in the USA, $46 billion[4] in relief aid is being sought. Contrast this response with the global commitment for malaria was US$2.7 billion in 2019[5]. May these funds do good and halt the devastation of both COVID-19 and malaria.

3   https://www.worldbank.org/en/news/press-release/2020/03/17/world-bank-group-increases-covid-19-response-to-14-billion-to-help-sustain-economies-protect-jobs

4   https://www.npr.org/2020/03/20/818471466/trump-administration-seeks-46-billion-for-agencies-to-deal-with-the-COVID19virus

5   https://www.who.int/news-room/fact-sheets/detail/malaria

The essential thing to keep in mind here is that each person who falls ill, no matter where in the world, is a human. Kindness treasures everyone equally.

> **Avoid:** Deprioritizing things you value.
>
> **Ask:** How can our actions create greater equity across what we value?
>
> **Do:** Appreciate that maintaining priorities in times of crisis is challenging.

IT IS HARD TO TRUST IN THE LEADERSHIP OF SOMEONE WHO IS HALF HEARTED ABOUT THEIR PURPOSE, OR ONLY SPORADIC IN FOCUS OR ENTHUSIASM.

—Sebastian Coe

WE RELISH NEWS OF OUR HEROS, FORGETTING THAT WE ARE EXTRAORDINARY TO SOMEONE TODAY.

—*Helen Hayes*

FAMILY AND THOSE WE LOVE

While some of us are facing the reality of distance and not being able to see those we love during a scary time, others are currently facing the challenge of having to spend 24/7 with family.

Which would you choose, if you could choose?

As for me, I'm thankful for **CISCO's** Webex, **Zoom**, **Skype** and my internet provider, **Singtel**. I'm in regular contact with home and on regular calls with friends all over. If there is one thing quarantine reminds me of, it's just how much I value the good people in my life.

Reach Out and Show You Care

With the stress of a global pandemic, the people we care about might be in a very different state of mind from us. Each country is dealing with a different set of issues, each is facing a different timeline. And yet, in a way, all of humanity is facing the same thing right now.

The reality of the human mind is that we are amazingly adaptable to new situations. Neuroplasticity is a beautiful thing. It keeps us learning and adapting successfully all our lives.

But in the short term, our initial response to something entirely new is a heady combination of anxiety, denial, and *it won't happen here*.

Then it does, and fear is calling the shots. It's real.

And when someone close to you is sick or in ICU, it is not easy being far away from them. One way to calm your fears is by calming someone else's—talk about instant karma! So, if you're feeling anxious, assume that the people you care about are feeling just as anxious and reach out to them.

Avoid: Pretending it's all fine. In reality, these are unusual times.

Ask: What can I do? When would be good to call?

Do: Reach out.

Even with all this fear, perhaps the kindest gift you can give someone is your love and your firm belief that all will be well, even if we don't quite know how.

ACCEPT THE THINGS TO WHICH FATE BINDS YOU, AND LOVE THE PEOPLE WHOM FATE BRING YOU TOGETHER WITH ALL YOUR HEART.

—Marcus Aurelius

Be Patient

We've a long game ahead of us. I wish I had a magic wand and could say it will all be gone soon, but after weathering SARS and other crises, I know there are stages to this.

Right now we've moved out of denial into to full realization that it's happening—and it's happening to us. This is where it gets a bit crazy.

Then crazy settles, if we give it a little space. We work out that we are here and alive. *Whew.* We rediscover ways to find joy. To laugh. We begin to spot flowers again.

Yes, there will be more challenging spaces, further twists and turns. But we are resilient creatures, particularly when we focus on kindness.

And if you have kids in the house, dealing with homeschooling them and all their energy—have fun. And be clear about the space you and they need to thrive, not just survive.

Avoid: Expecting it to be brilliant fast.

Ask: What would be cool today?

Do: Show up. Laughter is ok! Take one step forward today.

DO YOUR LITTLE BIT OF GOOD WHERE YOU ARE; IT'S THOSE LITTLE BITS OF GOOD PUT TOGETHER THAT OVERWHELM THE WORLD.

—Desmond Tutu

WHOEVER IS HAPPY WILL MAKE OTHERS HAPPY TOO.

—*Anne Frank*

SURVIVAL

Right now, survival is at the top of many minds. To keep things simple from the kindness perspective, let's look at survival across three areas.

- Yourself
- Those you love
- Your business

Each is going to face its own challenges.

Here is a structure that's helped me, my businesses, and my coaching clients deal with rapid change, uncertainty, and new opportunities. It's a success accelerator for turbulent times. It helps keep your focus on what you've decided is important. It helps you use the time and resources you have on hand in the best possible way.

This structure frames things within the Three Critical Perspectives.

Begin with what's important to you in the long run. This may be things that are already in your life and business. These may be the things you'd like to see transformed. This is the dark gray zone, the big picture, it's the transformation you want to see in the world, also known as Transform The Business, TTB, in the picture below.

Next, look at what you need to keep going, what's necessary to keep the lights on (KTLO). This is about the simple stuff. Bills that need to be paid. Promises to be honored. These are things that you need to do currently, not in six months. This is the small gray zone.

Then in the light gray zone in the middle, write down what you could do that would help you get to the big, transformed vision (TTB) faster. It's called grow the business (GTB).

THE THREE VALUABLE PERSPECTIVES

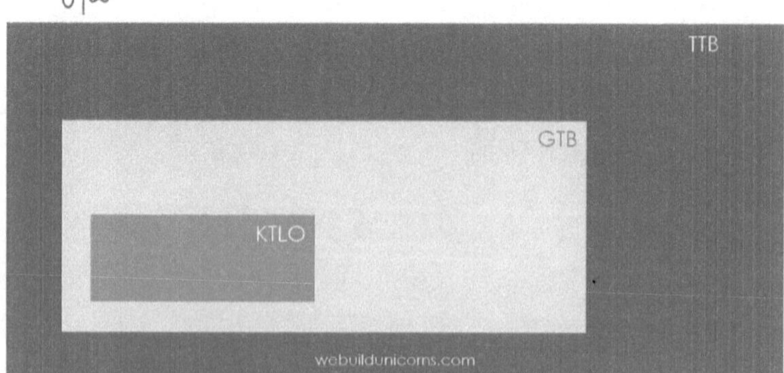

Draw this out and write down the things that are key for you for each perspective.

Have the backstops you need to be fine in place. That's the *keep the lights on* actions from Karma Action Point 22. After all, we have a roof over our head, food to eat, and something to do—even if it's as simple as curling up with a book, Netflixing, or having a conversation with a real live human . . . with appropriate social distancing, naturally.

HAPPINESS FUELS SUCCESS, NOT THE OTHER WAY AROUND.

—*Shawn Achor*

Kindness in Survival

This is actually a very powerful place for kindness. It's when you are deliberately using your mind and heart to do good, even if there is lots going on. It's like building a muscle.

If you've done the exercise I just shared, you'll have identified some things that are important to your survival in the *keep the lights on* space.

Now, apply the kindness principles to this. Given what you want, do you know someone who wants similar things? Look around.

Avoid: Going for the perfect person or over thinking this.

Ask: What could you do that is really meaningful for them, yet simple for you?

Do: Do it. Set up a meeting (virtual is fine) and help them.

The power of kindness is that it helps others. The beneficial side effect: it gets our attention off ourselves.

Kindness in Growth

When you are looking for what would help things grow, get better, or go faster, look for like-minded people or businesses with similar values. Find ways to partner with them and to amplify what they are doing. As you do this, their success will become your success.

In a time of crisis, this can be as simple as lending a helping hand or as meaningful as deliberately choosing to do a project that uses their skills (which helps them) to help you achieve what's important for you.

Avoid: Holding back and waiting for better. This is where you need to remember that small seeds create oak trees.

Ask: If I could get this started, would you be interested?

Do: Get started. Even if it's the first steps. It's progress.

Growth is really about progress. Grow exponentially as you help kindness go viral in unexpected ways.

MY MISSION IN LIFE IS NOT MERELY TO SURVIVE, BUT TO THRIVE; AND TO DO SO WITH SOME PASSION, SOME COMPASSION, SOME HUMOR AND SOME STYLE.

—Maya Angelou

Kindness for Transformation

This is where you focus on what would be magnificent. You are going to deliberately get out there to go for the big, fabulous vision.

When we are living in fear, this is tough. When we are living in possibility, it's actually relatively easy. Right now, fear and possibility walk hand in hand. We've all got 24 hours in a day, which is something the changes imposed on us by the coronavirus crisis does not change.

Once we've got the critical things covered, we may as well use time, our most precious resource—and often the scarcest—for good, to help others.

Magnificence, in Latin, is *magna fiacre*, which means to do the great work. What will your great work be? Think big, think magnificent, and most importantly, get started on it.

Kindness Is the Great Work

Here, focus on helping others be their greatest selves.

> **Avoid:** Playing small.
>
> **Ask:** If you could be the most magnificent version of you, what would it be like?
>
> **Do:** Listen respectfully, to their vision, even with a touch of awe.

If you are talking business, magnificence is every bit as relevant . . . what is the greatest good your business could create?

WHAT LIES BEHIND YOU AND WHAT LIES IN FRONT OF YOU, PALES INTO COMPARISON TO WHAT LIES INSIDE OF YOU.

—*Ralph Waldo Emerson*

I THANK YOU GOD FOR
THIS MOST AMAZING DAY,
FOR THE LEAPING GREENLY
SPIRITS OF TRESS, AND FOR
THE BLUE DREAM OF SKY
AND FOR EVERYTHING WITH
IS NATURAL, WHICH IS
INFINITE, WHICH IS YES.

—e e cummings

SUSTAINABILITY

One of the big takeaways from this global health crisis is how very connected we really are.

The climate crisis and the changes in weather we've faced lately showed us the truth that we are all connected—you, me, your people, your business, the world . . . the lot.

Now the spread of the novel coronavirus is hitting it home.

If we can find a way to deal with this crisis—and we will—we can also tackle the climate. We can do it fully, cleaning up the past.

In karmic terms, it's called clearing bad seeds. In business terms, it's about doing more than being climate neutral, which is an approach that still leaves us with the crap[6] that's in the system already, creating the climate crisis.

6   This is a technical term for all the messy stuff that needs to be cleaned up that we'd just as soon was not there but is. But as we are not ostriches with our heads in the sand, we can find ways. See it as an opportunity!

This is a big thing that will take enormous amounts of work to do justice on it. But right now, let's focus on the current crisis and recovery. Keep an eye out for *Climate Unicorning—5 Steps leaders can take to make sustainability profitable.*

LET US MAKE OUR FUTURE NOW, AND LET US MAKE OUR DREAMS TOMORROW'S REALITY.

—Malala Yousafzai

It Is One System

What we do today will come back to us. Let's deal with COVID-19 in a way that reduces waste and pollution. Let's see a recovery that cleans up the air, the water, and the land. One that keeps humans healthy by keeping plants and animals healthy too.

The kindness action here is about courage—courage to believe that each of us, and our businesses too, can and do make a difference.

> **Avoid:** Thinking you and your actions don't count.
>
> **Ask:** What difference can I make, even if it is small?
>
> **Do:** Commit to it. Keep doing it.

When I look at the Sustainable Development Goals and the Climate Reports, I wonder if we've been given this quarantine-induced surplus time to give thanks and to think about the world we want to have post-crisis. As leaders, we can and we must.

And we can commit to making the difference. We can begin to treat *everything* as one system—our system.

IT IS ALWAYS THE SIMPLE THAT PRODUCES THE MARVELOUS.

—*Amelia Barr*

MONEY

Money is one of our great creations, as human beings. It helps us share things, it helps us get things done halfway around the world, and it helps us on a rainy day. Right now, in the grip of a pandemic, how we relate to money is a litmus test for our future.

Much of this book has been focusing on the mindset and the heartset that will help you get through this crisis with more resilience. It's building a positive psychology for action that will accelerate your results as the recovery begins.

If fear is allowed to dominate, then money becomes the focus. Your mindset as a leader here is key.

Cash Flow

When times get tight, we hold our breath. In business, we want to hold onto our cash flow. But here's the thing: when we hold onto our cash flow, when we fail to deliver on the promises we've made, we are not being kind.

These actions contribute to the fear and the slowdown. They eventually put people out of jobs and businesses into that dark place that begins with b- and almost rhymes with "abruptly."

Truth be told, many parts of the economy will do just fine. Businesses that are prepared for ups and downs have services that work. When someone knows they will be paid, they get on with good work. It's survival psychology 101.

Now, for the CFOs reading this, remember that cash sitting in your war-chest *does nothing*. Value is not created. Value creation requires movement. This is called flow.

If you pay on time, others can pay you on time.

Be sensible. Look at the cash flow of your business and adjust. But do it in respectfulness to your existing promises. Do it in the spirit of looking after others.

After all, wouldn't you want the same kindness shown to you?

> **Avoid:** Paying late or dishonoring your word.
>
> **Ask:** How can we set up payment so it works for both of us?
>
> **Do:** Deliver on your cash promises.

The power of this came home to me back when my business at PricewaterhouseCoopers lost 90% of its cash flow during the Asian financial crisis. Cash was truly short. We worked with our clients, our partners, and our employees to figure out how we'd all get through. It required creative thinking, but we pulled it off in a way that was beneficial for everyone. The relationships, trust, and good-will such a course of action creates are the most valuable capital there is.

YOUR PRESENT CIRCUMSTANCES DON'T DETERMINE WHERE YOU CAN GO; THEY MERELY DETERMINE WHERE YOU START.

—Nido Qubein

Credit

Credit. Finance loves how it helps manage cash flow. It lets businesses get things done sooner than might otherwise be possible.

In the COVID-19 economic crisis, where cash flow is already becoming critical or negative for so many people and businesses, we can work with credit as an expression of trust and respect.

Giving credit is like giving appreciation. It compounds.

Asking for credit as a negotiation tactic based on power is something to be very wary of. For example, 180-day terms may kill the recipient. Even 90- or 30-day terms might be hard right now. Remember, kindness is about looking after the other side too, particularly if they are little guys.

Real-time exchange is great. Prepayment shows trust.

Avoid: Misusing power in these times.

Ask: What will work for you?

Do: Trust that what you need will come to you.

Note: *As part of the complex decision-making in disruption programs for the Chartered Professional Accountants (CPAs), I ask participants, "Would you like to be on the receiving end of this?" It's a simple test of do unto others what you'd like done unto you.*

Also note: The people and businesses with whom you interact will really appreciate that you are in a situation that allows you to pay now. They may be delighted and able to good things for you in the future, in that post-recovery world that we are building.

PEOPLE FIRST,
THE MONEY,
THEN THINGS.

—Suze Orman

A HERO IS SOMEONE WHO HAS GIVEN HIS OR HER LIFE TO SOMETHING BIGGER THAN ONESELF.

—Joseph Campbell

MEANING

The meaning we choose to give things is part of the fun of life. What looks like disaster to one person may be the opportunity of a lifetime for another. The current crisis is no different. So, put this to practical use. Decide on meanings that are helpful for you to move forward, rather than ones that hold you in a negative place.

For example, what if the coronavirus is a pause, like a summer break for us to ponder and let the air clear and for us to see what's important to us? What if it's a way for us to realize we can band together and, like a magnificence of unicorns (a magnificence is like a herd but only better), truly create a much better world? What if this is our opportunity to build things that will really help people and planet thrive?

This would be pretty cool. And we can give it that meaning if we choose to.

In light of a global tragedy, how do we pay homage to those who will no longer be with us when it's over? In their names, we build a better planet.

Trust in Good Intentions

Karma and kindness is about managing our mindset. At the base of it: when you trust the good intentions of others, it's amazing how often you are rewarded.

This is not naivety. The old wisdom that asked us to walk a mile in someone else's shoes was part of this. Understand where the other is coming from.

Seek to create solutions that serve the next level of results for you and for them.

Yes, bad stuff happens. But creating doubt and focusing on fear will slow down your ability to progress out of a situation that's not so great.

Avoid: Assuming ill will.

Ask: What positive reason may this person have for what they are doing?

Do: Take a moment to listen, to understand.

LOVE IS A FRUIT IN SEASON AT ALL TIMES, AND WITHIN REACH OF EVERY HAND.

—*Mother Teresa*

Watch Your Mind

Remember the sabre-tooth tiger test? It's that check that lets you know you are not in imminent physical danger. It's to calm your mind.

If you have developed a meditator's mind, that ability to watch your own mind and what it's up to, superb. Use it. Notice when it has its meltdowns. Keep breathing and kindly watch the emotions that are burbling up calm and settle.

If the paragraph above was gobble-di-gook for you, that's also ok. It was for me once, too. I had to learn to watch my mind. It was a bossy, destructive, always-on thing. In crisis, it would get busy imagining the worst, 99.9999% of which never happened.

Worry is a story in our mind. It's not about what is really happening right now, it's about the fears of what could be. Keep an eye on your mind, and if it goes into worry, firmly put your attention on something positive. For example, that vision you have in Karma Point 1. Rewrite the worry story with your hopes and desires in the starring role.

Avoid: Focusing on worry.

Ask: What is your vision and intention for a better future? Or a better today?

Do: Take a small, deliberate action towards this.

THE MEANING I PICKED, THE ONE THAT CHANGED MY LIFE: OVERCOME FEAR, BEHOLD WONDER.

—Richard Bach

SOMEONE IS SITTING IN THE SHADE TODAY BECAUSE SOMEONE PLANTED A TREE A LONG TIME AGO

—*Warren Buffet*

CAPITAL

If you've been in business growth, consulting, or the venture capital world, capital may be familiar territory to you. Over the last few decades, the rules of capital have changed, with these shifts accelerating greatly in the last decade.

While the venture capital and IPO world has gotten a lot of attention in the press, what we see is actually the result of a couple of changes:

- Technology and digitization created a whole new space for value creation
- IPO laws changed to allow more private investors (up to 2000)
- Quantitative easing during the GFC put $4 trillion into the US economy, which ultimately expands into $34 trillion (in other words, a whole lot more capital)

But before this, there was another trend, one that's key to the current crisis and recovery.

What is considered capital has changed, and what is considered valuable has changed too.

Back in the '80s, capital was primarily land, contracts, and cash. This is what the accounting profession recognized on the books.

These days, if you look at what the stock market values, 87% of market value comes from other assets.

In this crisis, looking after these forms of capitals is key.

The 87% that Counts Today

The assets that aren't land, contracts, or cash—the 87%—are where value is created today.

WHY: Possibilities are what you are able to create and deliver on. The COVID-19 crisis is creating plenty of these.

WHEN: More than ever, your ability to get a product to market in an appropriate time is of the essence. During a pandemic, this may mean holding off on some services while accelerating others.

WHAT: Your brand is about the values you hold and the promises you make to your customers, suppliers, and the world. We are in a world that values integrity and can see through to falsehood. The current crisis only heightens the importance of these principles.

WHO: Your relationships and networks are about trust and access. Relationships with trust move faster. Networks reduce search cost. Together they accelerate collaboration and results, so essential for confronting today's challenges.

HOW: Your technology, processes, and intellectual property help things get done faster. They save re-inventing the wheel, the chip, and even single-click purchasing.

In the midst of the coronavirus crisis, identify which of these assets are relevant and important to you and your vision—and make sure your look after them. As things move forward, look at this Karma Action Point along with Karma Action Points #22, #23 and #24. They will help you and your people stay focused and make progress for a swifter recovery.

Avoid: Getting bogged down with trying to do it all.

Ask: Which assets are critical for our future, and what is next?

Do: Look after your key strengths.

AS FAR AS SERVICE GOES, IT CAN TAKE THE FORM OF A MILLION THINGS.

—Elsabeth Kubler-Ross

**WELL, YOU KNOW,
I WAS A HUMAN BEING
BEFORE I BECAME A
BUSINESSMAN.**

—*George Soros*

The Traditional 13%

The traditional 13% of assets are still important. Maintain awareness of cash flow. Contracts, money, and physical property are all part of the physical world. In the current crisis, look after them.

Avoid: Burning and wasting your traditional assets.

Ask: What can we do to preserve the value of our assets?

Do: Put action in place to protect those assets.

IT IS NEVER TOO LATE TO BE WHAT YOU MIGHT HAVE BEEN.

—George Eliot

COMPASSION

Crises are trying times. They bring out the best and the worst in us. In the social distancing, in the isolation, in the lockdowns, and in the police and military presence required to manage the impact of COVID-19, we are truly facing the unknown.

This is where our sense of compassion (*to feel with*—yes! Latin skills score again ☺) is key. Kindness is a path of compassion. Each of our Karma Action Points are about compassion.

Remember: we can chose how we feel, we can help others, and we can create a better world.

Empathy

The superpower of kindness is empathy. Kindness is about others. Karma in Action is founded on the golden rule of doing for others what you'd like done for you. Karma in Action asks you to give in order to receive.

The more you do and repeat the simple actions in this book, the more your mind will be under your control and you will be free to act for good.

Empathy is a force for good.

Avoid: Letting the opportunity pass.

Ask: What can I do right now to help you?

Do: Take action with a lightness of spirit.

THE BEST AND MOST BEAUTIFUL THINGS IN THE WORLD CANNOT BE SEEN OR EVEN TOUCHED – THEY MUST BE FELT WITH THE HEART.

—Helen Keller

MAGNIFICENCE IS YOU.

—Joanne Flinn

You At Your Best

Some say that we are only ever given challenges that we are capable of facing. COVID-19 and even the climate crisis are challenges we can face. You at your best is able to do the magnificent, to create the better future.

And each time you deliberately take a karmic action, take note of it. As you go to sleep reflect on the good you've done today.

This is your call to magnificence.

Avoid: Running away.

Ask: If I could do anything, what would I do?

Do: Help someone else realize their dreams, too.

KINDNESS IS THE WIND BENEATH YOUR WINGS.

—Booth Aster

KINDNESS

This crisis is asking new things of us. It's creating new opportunities for kindness to those nearest us, and novel opportunities to do good.

For example:

A fortnight ago when I was coming out of that ICU I mentioned at the beginning of this book, a friend called to see how I was. This was a kindness. She then suggested that we dedicate 48 hours over the next two weekends to doing good, to putting our skills and talents to use to help you.

Our goal: to both write short, practical eBooks to inspire and help people through these times.

She's an expert in taking on challenges creatively. Sonja Piontek's book is UltraCreativity – The Experiment.

As you've seen, mine is about business transformation, that complex combination of people, passion, and cash. The key to any change, to any success, is first to get your mindset and heartset fixed on the future, and then to go create it.

May these 33 Karma Action Points bring you calm, may they bring you capacity, and above all, may they help you create the better future magnificently!

> **Avoid:** Just passively reading!
>
> **Ask:** Who can I share this with?
>
> **Do:** Go share it.

You can find about Karma in action for yourself, your team or your business, at www.KarmaInAction.works

About the Author

Joanne Flinn, the Business Growth Lady, ran her first $10 million dollar business at 23 before going on to lead Financial Services Consulting at PricewaterhouseCoopers during the Asian financial crisis, she then went on to the IT ExCo at a major Asian bank and dealt with SARS with teams across Asia. These days, she is a co-founder of the Change Leaders, a global professional community focusing what creates success during disruption. Joanne holds an MSC in Consulting and Coaching for Change from HEC Paris and Saïd Business School at the University of Oxford.

Twice a TEDx speaker, she's published five books on different elements of change, transformation, and digital disruption.

Acknowledgements

Putting a book together takes effort, it takes the background knowledge, it definitely takes reflection. Without these, I'd not have been able to say yes to Sonja Piontek's thoughtful challenge.

I thank the clients who have trusted me with their visions. You gave me the space to put the heart and the logic together for what's become *Karma in Action* and what, when the time is right, will become *Unicorning*. We do truly have the power to do the magnificent and create a better future.

Thanks also to my dear friends Andrea T Edwards, Lavinia Thanapathy, and Louisa Bennion. You got me back into the book process; you trusted me to get important messages out and to get books done.

And to Alice Flinn Stilwell—thank you for trusting that it would all be ok, when I got on a plane in the midst of a pandemic. It is, and it will be.